IDENTITY

every

teenager

should

know

NEW HOPE®
PUBLISHERS
Imprint of Iron Stream Media

Birmingham, Alabama

Other books in the
31 Verses Every Teenager Should Know series:

Love	*Inhabit*	*Character*	*Prime*
Rooted	*Sequence*	*Community*	*Reverb*
The Way	*Christ*	*Linked*	

New Hope® Publishers
100 Missionary Ridge
Birmingham, AL 35242
NewHopePublishers.com
An imprint of Iron Stream Media
IronStreamMedia.com

Title: Identity : 31 verses every teenager should know.
Description: First [edition]. | Birmingham : New Hope Publishers, 2019.
Identifiers: LCCN 2019012558 | ISBN 9781563092732 (permabind)
Subjects: LCSH: Identity (Psychology)--Religious aspects--Christianity. | Christian teenagers--Religious life.
Classification: LCC BV4509.5 .I34 2019 | DDC 242/.63--dc23
LC record available at https://lccn.loc.gov/2019012558

ISBN-13: 978-1-56309-273-2
Ebook ISBN: 978-1-56309-274-9

1 2 3 4 5—23 22 21 20 19

Contents

Who Do You Think You Are?

Here's a question: Who are you?

What defines your identity?

What makes you different from your friends and family? What about you makes you stand out among the billions of other people on this planet? It can't just be your personality or your interests. It can't just be your talents or your passions. And it can't just be your appearance. Why? Because all of these things change over time.

Face it. You may not always be the smartest or most talented person. You may not always be able to do the things you can do today. Personalities change. Your appearance definitely will.

So what makes you, well . . . *you*?

I want to offer a suggestion about the nature of who you are . . . an answer to the question, What defines your identity? I believe God's Word makes it clear. If you are a Christ follower, then your identity is found in Christ. Simple as that.

All the questions about your value, your purpose, your appearance, and your self-worth are answered in Christ. You are who you are because He is who He is. Christ is your advocate, your healer, your friend, your master, and your Savior.

But don't take my word for it. Let God's Word speak for itself.

That really is my challenge to you. I wrote this book to try to show you all the wonderful things the Bible says about the nature of your identity. My prayer is that through reading it, you will learn more about Christ and learn more about yourself in relation to Him. I hope you find that God's Word speaks to you through each of these pages and that your passion to know Christ is ignited.

How to Use This Book

Now that you own this incredible little book, you may be wondering, "What do I do with it?"

Glad you asked. The great thing about this book is you can use it just about any way you want.

It's not a system. It's a resource that can be used in ways that are as unique and varied as you are.

A few suggestions . . .

The One-Month Plan

On this plan, you'll read one devotional each day for a month. This is a great way to immerse yourself in the Bible for a month-long period. (Okay, we realize every month doesn't have thirty-one days. But twenty-eight or thirty is close enough to thirty-one, right?) The idea is to cover a lot of information in a short amount of time.

The Scripture Memory Plan

The idea behind this plan is to memorize the verse for each day's devotional; you don't move on to the next devotional until you have memorized the Scripture you're on. If you're like most people, this might take you more than one day per devotional. So this plan takes a slower approach.

The "I'm No William Shakespeare" Plan

Don't like to write or journal? This plan is for you. Listen, not everyone expresses themselves the same way. If you don't like to express yourself through writing, that's okay. Simply read the devotional for each verse, then read the questions. Think about them. Pray through them. But don't feel like you have to journal if you don't want to.

The Strength in Numbers Plan

God designed humans for interaction. We are social creatures. How cool would it be if you could go through *Identity* with your friends? Get a group of friends together. Consider agreeing to read five verses each week, then meeting to talk about it.

Pretty simple, right? Choose a plan. Or make up your own. But get started already. What are you waiting on?

Verse 1

Therefore, if anyone is in Christ, the new creation has come: The old has gone, the new is here!

—2 Corinthians 5:17

New creations excite people. This is true for a lot of different reasons. Take a creation such as the pacemaker. A pacemaker is a device implanted inside an individual that helps control that person's heart rate. If you were struggling with heart problems, this creation would get you pumped. (Get it? *Pumped?*) If you're like me, new gadgets excite you; I always look forward to the newest creations the folks at Apple dream up. If you're a gamer, new games excite you. If you're a musician, new songs or arrangements excite you. If you're a skater, new tricks excite you. If you're a football player, new plays excite you. For most people the idea of something totally new is pretty cool.

Read 2 Corinthians 5:16–19. Second Corinthians was written by the Apostle Paul to the church in Corinth he helped found. But the church had been a source of frustration to Paul; they seemed to struggle mightily with their spiritual growth. Paul spent a great deal of time trying to help them stay on the right track with God. In this passage he was more or less speaking to the way followers of Christ should look at others. Paul wanted his readers to see that people who have committed themselves to Christ are different. How are they different? Well, the answer to that question is the key to understanding your identity in Christ.

Paul wrote that people who submit their lives to Christ's lordship literally become something new. There is a change. Whoever they were, with their faults and wants and sin, is gone. In the place of those things is life, and hope, and purpose. In the place of their flaws, there is Christ.

Rejoice that you are a new creation in Christ. Understanding this truth is the first step in grasping your true identity in Christ.

Think about your life as a Christ follower. When do you first remember submitting your will to Jesus?

_____

_____

_____

_____

What does it mean to you to live as a new creation in the world around you?

_____

_____

_____

_____

Define your identity. How has being a Christ follower affected your identity?

_____

_____

_____

_____

Verse 2

Your hands made me and formed me; give me understanding to learn your commands.

—Psalm 119:73

If you've ever watched someone make something out of clay, you know it can be pretty cool to see something emerge out of nothing. Maybe you've seen a potter crafting objects out of a raw, earth-colored mass. Or maybe it's simply a little kid making something out of a colorful pile of Play-Doh. Maybe you're a sculptor yourself. Whatever the case may be, it's amazing to see a lump of clay formed into a bowl, or a vase, or a flower, or an abstract work of art. Where there was once something formless, in its place is a new creation.

Read Psalm 119:73–80. Pay close attention to verse 73. Because here you see the foundation of your identity. Quite simply, you couldn't be who you are you if you had not been created in the first place. Does God craft each person in the world by hand, one at a time? Does He have a large pile of supernatural human clay that he forms babies out of? Of course not. But that's not really the point of the verse. The author of Psalm 119 is using imagery to speak to the fact that your life originates with God.

Psalm 119:73 firmly establishes God as the source of your life. You did not happen by accident. You are literally alive because God chose to create you. He did not have to. You certainly did not earn it. He formed you Himself and created you intentionally. You can be who you are because God saw fit to create you.

As you begin to think about the source of your identity, you can never forget that you were created to be a part of God's creation.

How does the statement, you are alive because God wanted you to be in this world, make you feel?

_____

_____

_____

_____

What does knowing that God intentionally created you do for the way you value yourself?

_____

_____

_____

_____

What does this truth say about your life on this earth? If God made you, how should you use your life?

_____

_____

_____

_____

Verse 3

Listen to me, you islands; hear this, you distant nations: Before I was born the LORD called me; from my mother's womb he has spoken my name.

—Isaiah 49:1

What is your name? Is it a relatively common name, like John or Sarah? Maybe you're one of the lucky ones whose name has some real flair . . . like Alejandro or Caldonia or Santosha. Names are significant. And some are more significant than others. My oldest daughter is named after both of her grandmothers. For her, a name is a reminder of the character of the women she is named after and the love they have for her. Maybe you share the name of a cherished family member too.

Read Isaiah 49:1–4. Isaiah was one of God's chosen messengers. These messengers, called *prophets*, spoke to God's people. Sometimes their message was encouraging. Sometimes it was harsh. But they were called to be the Lord's obedient servants. In verse 1 Isaiah said God called him to this duty before he was even born. Isaiah saw himself as an arrow in the Lord's quiver to be used to shoot a message of truth right in the hearts of God's people. Isaiah knew the source of his identity and purpose.

Don't miss the imagery in verse 1. Isaiah said that before he was even born, the Lord "spoke his name." Amazing! The name Isaiah was on God's lips before the man was even alive.

Your name is on God's lips too. It has been on His lips since the beginning of time. You see, God is eternal. He has always been. He will always be. And His plans are unchanging. God's plan for us, His people, was set forth before time. And that plan included you. How awesome is that?

Say your name out loud. For real. Say it. Say it again. That name has been on God's lips since before you took your first breath. God knew your identity before you did.

Can you imagine God saying your name? How does knowing God cares for you so personally affect the way you view Him?

_____

_____

_____

_____

Go look up the origins of your name online—maybe on a baby name website. What does it mean? Does it describe you accurately?

_____

_____

_____

_____

God included you as part of His plan. How does that make you feel?

_____

_____

_____

_____

Verse 4

So God created mankind in his own image, in the image of God he created them; male and female he created them.

—Genesis 1:27

If you were to be really honest (Which you totally can be. I won't tell anyone. Promise.), you would probably admit that there have been times when you've felt pretty worthless. I know for some of you this may happen pretty regularly. For others, maybe these occasional moments of self-doubt are caused by relationships or circumstances. I know there have been moments in my life when I've looked in the mirror and wondered if I really had anything to offer. While these feelings are not healthy, they are pretty common. They can leave us feeling quite low.

Want a pick-me-up? Read Genesis chapter 1. (Yes, the whole thing.) Pay close attention to verses 26 and 27. Do you see what those verses say? They say two things. One, that God created you. Two, that you were created in His image. What does that mean? Glad you asked . . . It means you are a reflection of God's character and personality. And the source of how you act and think and feel is how God acts and thinks and feels. Because you were made in His likeness, in His image, you reflect a glimmer of Him to the world.

So how does this change your day-to-day life? Quite powerfully, actually. Because being made in God's image means you were not a mistake. You were not an afterthought. You matter. You are not worthless. You are worth everything to the Creator of the universe. Your identity, your worth, your value, and your beauty are based solely on the fact that you were crafted in the likeness of God.

Don't ever, ever, *ever* let the world beat you down. You are God's handcrafted treasure, lovingly made to reflect Himself. *This* is your identity.

If you struggle with feelings of doubt or low self-image, have you looked to Scripture to find evidence of God's love for you? How can you give God the chance to show you how much you are worth to Him?

_____

_____

_____

What does it mean to you that you are a reflection of God to the world?

_____

_____

_____

How does being made in God's image affect your obedience to Him?

_____

_____

_____

Verse 5

I will take you as my own people, and I will be your God.

—Exodus 6:7

Think for a moment about your prized possessions, those belongings you hold most dear. These look different for each of us. For one of you reading this, your prized possession might be a quilt your grandmother made for you when you were a baby. For others it might be an autographed baseball, vintage vinyl, your new iPhone, or even your car. My prized possession is an electric guitar. And because it is important to me, I place great value on it. I treat it differently from the way I treat my lawnmower.

Read Exodus 6:6–8. God was preparing to do great things through Moses. The Israelites, God's people, had been enslaved in Egypt for four hundred years. God was about to act on His promise to be His people's deliverer. As you read this passage, look how many times God says, "I will." God is showing Moses He is a God of action. Each "I will" is a promise. And God proved faithful to His people. He did ultimately bring them out of slavery and deliver them to the Promised Land.

Read verse 7 again. God describes His relationship with the Israelites in such great terms. He sets up a one-to-one relationship: the Israelites are His people, and He is their God.

The Israelites were God's prized possessions. And you know what? You are a direct spiritual descendant of the Israelites through Jesus Christ. Jesus came so that all of God's people might enjoy this wonderful one-to-one relationship. You are a part of the larger family of God's chosen ones.

You are God's prized possession. He is your God. You are His people. What an amazing privilege.

How does the privilege of being one of God's children affect your identity?

_____

_____

_____

_____

_____

_____

List some ways you utilize the one-to-one relationship you have with God.

_____

_____

_____

_____

_____

Write a prayer to God thanking Him for sending His Son so that you might be identified as one of His children.

_____

_____

_____

_____

_____

Verse 6

I have been crucified with Christ and I no longer live, but Christ lives in me. The life I now live in the body, I live by faith in the Son of God, who loved me and gave himself for me.

—Galatians 2:20

Think about your identity. What makes you who you are? If you think about it, you aren't really any one thing. You are a collection of a lot of different things: your talents, personality, weaknesses, strengths, likes, dislikes, appearance, desires, needs, and habits. You're kind of like a mash-up, but instead of combining two or more songs to make one song, you are the combination of all these little things. What's the end result? Your identity.

Read Galatians 2:15–21. The Apostle Paul wrote Galatians to address some issues in the church of Galatia. People were trying to mislead the Christ followers, and Paul was urgently trying to straighten out the Galatians. In verses 20 and 21 Paul unveils the truth about the nature of our relationship with Christ. Paul defines the source of his spiritual strength and gives a glimpse into what defined his identity.

Think back to how we defined your identity. When Paul says, "I have been crucified with Christ and I no longer live," he is talking about his identity. Literally, all the things that made Paul who he was (his identity) were put to death when he submitted his life to Christ. And in the place of the dead identity, a new one was born. Here's the real key: This new identity is the identity of Christ living in Paul.

We all project an identity to the world. But if you are a Christ follower, something wonderful and mysterious has happened: your old identity has died, and your new identity in Christ is being refined each day. Each day you walk with the Lord is another day you project Him into the world. Christ lives in you. Living for Him is the source of your identity as a believer.

Your old self has been crucified with Christ. It is dead. Are there any habits or attitudes that you haven't buried yet?

_____

_____

_____

_____

What will it take for you to bury the habits or attitudes that still linger from your old self?

_____

_____

_____

_____

How are you showing the world around you that Christ in you influences your identity?

_____

_____

_____

_____

Verse 7

On that day you will realize that I am in my Father, and you are in me, and I am in you.

—John 14:20

There are times in life when we need to be comforted. People die. Friends turn their backs. Dreams crash and burn. These times can be unbearable. One of the best ways to get through life's low points is leaning on other people. When you experience pain or loss or frustration, it pays to allow good friends or family to provide some comfort. In these times of need, the right people are a huge resource.

Read John 14:15–21. This is a promise that cuts through history, providing comfort and reassurance today even as it did two thousand years ago. Jesus was promising His followers the gift of the Holy Spirit. Jesus said when He would leave this world to return to heaven, He would send the Spirit to dwell inside every believer. Jesus basically said, "When you see all this happen, you'll finally get all of this stuff I have been saying." Jesus was helping His followers see that once His earthly life ended, they would finally understand Jesus was who He said He was.

Jesus knew His followers would realize that He was one with the Father. But more than that, Jesus knew we would understand that we are in Him and He is in us. Do you understand the significance of this? Jesus has gathered you to Himself. Jesus has your identity wrapped up in His own. And His identity is wrapped up in you. You are joined with Jesus Christ, the Son of God. And nothing can separate this union.

You are in Jesus. He is in you. When the storms of life rage around you, remember this truth. It is a crucial part of your identity and part of Jesus' eternal promise to His children.

Can you think of a time when good friends or family helped you out in a struggle?

_____

_____

_____

_____

Describe how that made you feel.

_____

_____

_____

_____

How is God able to help you out in your time of need?

_____

_____

_____

_____

How is your outlook on life different because Christ is in you?

_____

_____

_____

_____

Verse 8

Rather, clothe yourselves with the Lord Jesus Christ,
and do not think about how to gratify the desires of
the flesh.

—Romans 13:14

Each morning you do something pretty simple, the significance of which you probably take for granted. Every morning you get dressed. See, told you it was simple. But seriously, getting dressed is kind of important, right? I mean, what's the alternative? *Not* getting dressed? Even though you'd probably be a lot more well-known in your school, not getting dressed presents some problems. For one thing, you would be quite unready to meet the world. Clothing yourself is a crucial part of going about your day.

Read Romans 13:11–14. The Apostle Paul was writing to the Christians in Rome. In this particular passage, Paul encouraged them to live as people who fully embrace their identities as Christ followers. The Roman culture was one of the crudest, most explicit cultures in the history of the world. That's why Paul challenged his readers to stay away from the horrible practices of the culture (sex, drunkenness, etc.) and to embrace their identity as followers of Christ. Paul used a great image to help his readers understand: the image of putting on their clothes.

No person would leave his or her house without being fully clothed. Your clothes prepare you for your day. Plus, your clothes tell people who you are. What would it take for you to wake up each morning and clothe yourself with Christ? First, just as you deliberately choose what to wear, choose to follow Christ today. Then, in the same way you take great care to make sure your clothes are presentable, evaluate your actions and thoughts to make sure you are on the same page with the Lord. Then, greet the world, confident that you are representing Christ to the culture around you.

Clothing yourself in Christ is the absolute best way to prepare to engage the world. Give it a shot. You won't be disappointed.

How do your clothes communicate your personality to the world?

_____

_____

_____

_____

What would it look like for you to go about the process of clothing yourself in Christ today?

_____

_____

_____

_____

How does the world know you are a Christ follower?

_____

_____

_____

_____

Verse 9

And we, who with unveiled faces contemplate the Lord's glory, are being transformed into his image with ever-increasing glory, which comes from the Lord, who is the Spirit.

—2 Corinthians 3:18

When I think of the word *transformation*, the first thing I think of is the killer action movie franchise *Transformers*. Maybe for you it's different. Do you think about the transformation that takes place on some of the reality TV shows like *The Biggest Loser* or *Fixer Upper*? If you're an actor, you might think about the crazy transformation that happens when characters get in costume to play roles like Lord Voldemort in *Harry Potter*. One of the reasons we are so intrigued by the idea of transformation is because we see this new, separate thing emerge from something totally different.

Read 2 Corinthians 3:12–18. The Apostle Paul wrote to the Corinthians, who could be a little bit of a pain. For every step forward they seemed to take in their spiritual growth, they took two steps back. In this passage, Paul reminded them of Moses. When Moses would come down from talking with God on top of the mountain, his face would be glowing. Being in God's presence produced this glow. So Moses would cover his face to keep from frightening the people. Soon, the glow would fade away, and he would remove the veil.

Because you are a follower of Christ, you reflect God's glory. The world sees your glow and recognizes something different about you. They should. You know why? Because you are literally being transformed each day into the likeness of Christ. Isn't that incredible? You are growing to look more like Jesus in your actions, thoughts, and words.

Your identity is transforming into *His* identity . . . a little more each day. How cool is that?

_____

_____

_____

What things can you do to ensure you are daily growing into Christ's likeness?

_____

_____

_____

What things can you do that might inhibit your growth?

_____

_____

_____

As you grow in Christ's likeness, how will your effect on the world around you change? What do you think it will do to your "glow"?

_____

_____

_____

Verse 10

We are therefore Christ's ambassadors, as though God were making his appeal through us. We implore you on Christ's behalf: Be reconciled to God.

—2 Corinthians 5:20

Eric and Travis were best friends. Until Eric did something very, very un-cool. Eric knew Travis had a ridiculous crush on Trish. So when Eric asked Trish to homecoming, it pretty much killed his friendship with Travis. Eric felt horrid, so he went to Trish and told her everything: how Travis had a huge crush on her and that even though Eric liked her, there was no way they could go to the dance after all. Then Eric went to Travis and told him what he'd done, that he'd back out of the date with Trish because his friendship with Travis meant too much. Travis wasn't ready to talk that night. But early the next morning, Eric got a text from Travis: *We're cool*. And that was that. Eric and Travis were buds again.

Read 2 Corinthians 5:16–21. The Apostle Paul was talking to the Corinthians about their calling as Christ followers. He explained to them that they had a mission: to help the world understand that God longed to be in a relationship with His children. God sent Jesus to die for our sins. You see, Jesus was perfect. So when Jesus, God's Son, was murdered simply for being who He said He was, God looked at Jesus' death on the Cross as payment for the sins of all God's children. This payment reconciled us to God.

What does *reconciled* mean? And why are you an ambassador of it? Well, reconciliation is what took place between Travis and Eric. When two people are reconciled, they are brought back together, and whatever tore them apart is forgiven. God has brought His people back to Him. The sins of all Christ followers have been forgiven. Through the blood of Jesus, all who believe have been united with God. Know what? Your calling is to tell the world this amazing fact.

Part of your identity is the role of ambassador. You are tasked with telling the world about Christ.

You are Jesus' ambassador. An ambassador is someone who represents another person's interests when that person is not around. How do you feel about the responsibility of being Christ's ambassador?

_____

_____

_____

_____

In your own words, how did Jesus reconcile the world to Him? How can you communicate your answer to the world around you?

_____

_____

_____

_____

Verse 11

That is why, for Christ's sake, I delight in weaknesses, in insults, in hardships, in persecutions, in difficulties. For when I am weak, then I am strong.

—2 Corinthians 12:10

All around the world, everyday, people are being murdered because they are Christ followers. Killed. Teenagers like you. Young adults like me. Yet in our churches and youth groups we talk about persecution in terms of our discomfort. We'll say, "Being a Christian might make you unpopular." Or, "Being a Christian might mean you get left out of parties." Or, "Being a Christian might mean you get made fun of." And we pass this off as persecution. Meanwhile, a Saudi Arabian teenage girl is murdered by her Muslim father because she converted to Christianity.

Read 2 Corinthians 12:7–10. The Apostle Paul knew what it meant to be persecuted. He was beaten, stoned, whipped, imprisoned . . . all for the sake of Christ. But look what he wrote in verse 10: he viewed all the hardships he faced for Christ as joy. You see, Paul knew his life on this earth was being used for Christ. While the trials he went through were terrible, he had the right perspective. In his moment of trial, he went from one who was weak to one who was strong. He took on the strength of Christ.

So here's the deal. I didn't launch into my whole persecution spiel to make you feel guilty. If anything, the freedom we have in the United States should make us thankful . . . every day. But if there are teenagers around the world willing to give everything for Christ, what is keeping you from living that way today? Paul knew that when he was persecuted because of Christ, Christ became stronger in Him. Don't you want to know that? I do.

Live a life today that tells the world you are identified with Christ, regardless of the consequences.

Why are you sometimes afraid to take a stand for Christ?

_____

_____

_____

_____

If you truly believe the Bible, why is it so important for your identity to be wrapped up in telling the world about Jesus?

_____

_____

_____

_____

What will it take for you to live radically for Jesus in your world without fearing what people think of you?

_____

_____

_____

_____

Verse 12

For to me, to live is Christ and to die is gain.

—Philippians 1:21

Let's play a game. I am going to throw out a few different words. You respond by writing one-word descriptions out beside them. For example, if I say "country music," you might say, "Awful." (Or, "Amazing," depending on your taste.) You get the idea? Let's do it:

Ariana Grande	_____
Taco Bell	_____
Your hairstyle	_____
Spotify	_____
Asparagus	_____
Social Media	_____
Your brother or sister	_____

Now, that was pretty fun. (Man, I wish I could see your answers. Especially how you responded to Taco Bell . . . *mmmmmmm*.) One-word descriptions can be powerful, right? They force you to say exactly what you mean. Read Philippians 1:15–21. The Apostle Paul wrote this letter to the Philippian church from his prison in Rome. Paul had been jailed because he preached Christ.

What Paul wrote in verse 21 is nothing short of remarkable. Paul used the same kind of one-word description you used earlier. Except Paul was describing his life, and he used the most powerful word possible: Christ. Paul lived in such a manner that his life, his identity, could be described by the word Christ! His life was so identified with Jesus, the very character of Christ described the way Paul lived. Wow! That is amazing . . . what a statement.

How amazing it would be if the people around you could examine your life and say, "Christ." Make that your goal today. Live for Christ.

What if people around you were asked to describe your life with one word? What would they say?

_____

_____

_____

_____

Describe the kind of commitment it takes to live in such a bold way.

_____

_____

_____

_____

If you were honest with yourself, how would you finish this sentence: For me, to live is _____.

_____

_____

_____

_____

Verse 13

Follow God's example, therefore, as dearly loved children.

—Ephesians 5:1

I love to work with my hands. I like painting, wood carving, and building stuff. One of the coolest things I've ever built is a playhouse for my daughters. It's pretty sweet, if I do say so myself. Part of the fun of building it was having my daughters hang out with me while I was working. My middle child would watch me and copy what I was doing. If I measured wood, she measured wood. If I used the level, she would pick it up and imitate what I was doing. It didn't matter that she didn't quite understand all the details; she was just imitating her dad. Maybe you have similar stories from your childhood.

Read Ephesians 5:1–10. The church in Ephesus was one of the Apostle Paul's favorite churches. It's no wonder the Book of Ephesians is a tender letter; we can almost feel Paul's affection for his friends there. In this particular passage, Paul was trying to guide his friends in righteous living. Look at how he led them in verses 3 through 6. He was challenging them to live rightly.

Paul gave his friends a pretty exhaustive list of things to do and not to do. But if we look at verse 1, I think we'll find a pretty simple bit of advice on how to make sure we are living according to God's commands. Quite simply, Paul said, "Follow God's example." In other words, we are to imitate God. What a cool way to think about our identity in Christ: God imitators. Are you a God imitator? Think about that concept as you go throughout your day.

What would it take for you to imitate God today?

_____

_____

_____

_____

_____

When we are not living rightly, who or what are we imitating?

_____

_____

_____

_____

_____

When you imitate God, what impact do you have on those around you?

_____

_____

_____

_____

_____

Verse 14

But now he has reconciled you by Christ's physical body through death to present you holy in his sight, without blemish and free from accusation.

—Colossians 1:22

We've all heard the dramatic stories of the wrongly accused. In a tragic failure of justice, someone is found guilty of a crime they did not commit. They are tried, found guilty, and imprisoned. Until the last twenty years or so, this would have been the end of it. Sure, they would have had the right to appeal, but few appeals ever result in a case being overturned. Enter DNA testing. Nowadays, the number of wrongly accused is falling thanks to DNA testing. Even more interesting is the number of people who have been released from prison because DNA testing proved their innocence.

Can you imagine what it must feel like to be freed from prison, to have your name cleared, to be absolved of all wrongdoing? Well, you don't have to think that hard. You're closer to the experience than you might realize.

Read Colossians 1:15–23. Paul wrote from prison in Rome. In his letter to the Colossians, Paul penned one of the most dynamic descriptions of Christ in the entire Bible. But pay attention to Colossians 1:22. Do you notice anything there that relates to this devotion's introduction?

As you think of your identity in Christ, think about this: you stand innocent in the presence of God. Christ has purchased your innocence with His blood shed on the Cross. You are free from guilt in God's eyes. Now, you will sin. You will fall short. It is our curse as humans. But because of what Jesus Christ did for you on the Cross, you are not accused of a crime in God's court. You stand free of accusation.

Part of your identity in Christ is your innocence before God. Have you thanked Jesus for this lately?

_____

_____

_____

What does it mean to be without blemish? Knowing your innermost thoughts and desires, can you imagine yourself this way?

_____

_____

_____

What does it do to the way you approach your relationship with Christ to know He has made you innocent?

_____

_____

_____

Write a short prayer to Christ thanking Him for taking away the guilt of your sins.

_____

_____

_____

Verse 15

For you died, and your life is now hidden with Christ in God.

—Colossians 3:3

Do you study a foreign language? If so, what language is it? Is it French? *Parlez-vous français?* Is it German? *Sprechen Sie Deutsch?* Or, maybe it's Swedish. *Talar du svenska?* There are certainly a lot of options. But I am willing to bet that while you might be taking a foreign language in school, it's not Greek. Am I right?

Actually, Greek is pretty important. You see, the New Testament was more or less written in Greek. And sometimes, by looking at the original Greek, a passage takes on a new meaning. Today's devotion is one of those passages. So it's foreign language time! (Don't everyone cheer at once . . .)

Read Colossians 3:1–11. What a cool passage. Again, Paul wrote from prison in Rome. He wanted the Colossian Christians to have a solid idea of who Christ is and what it takes to follow Him. In verse 3 Paul included this amazing statement. He wrote that our lives are hidden with Christ in God. Let's focus on that word *hidden*.

The Greek word translated *hide* is *krypto*. Its primary verb form is used much like we use the word *hide* today. But in Colossians 3:3, the word *krypto* is emphasizing the security we have in Christ. Think about it: Would you dare walk up to God without being completely covered by Christ? I wouldn't. I couldn't! There's no way I could face God without Christ standing in for me. So here we see this great word *hidden* used to describe our safety in Christ.

Isn't it amazing . . . the more you learn about your identity in Christ, the more you realize how much He has done for you. He is worthy of your praise.

How does being hidden in Christ affect the way you approach God in prayer?

_____

_____

_____

_____

How does being hidden in Christ affect the way you approach God in worship?

_____

_____

_____

_____

How does being hidden in Christ affect the way you approach God in service?

_____

_____

_____

_____

Verse 16

What is more, I consider everything a loss because of the surpassing worth of knowing Christ Jesus my Lord, for whose sake I have lost all things. I consider them garbage, that I may gain Christ.

—Philippians 3:8

I am a Red Sox fan. A big one. My allegiance is rooted in my earliest sports memories. I was nine years old in 1986 when a young pitcher named Roger Clemens set a major league record by striking out twenty batters in one game. Let's just say that got my attention. Then, in the last inning of game six of the 1986 World Series, Boston's first baseman let a ball go between his legs that cost the Sox the game and the Series. It's been called the closest any team ever came to winning a championship without actually winning it. The loss was agonizing. And I was hooked. I've been a fan ever since.

Read Philippians 3:7–10. Philippians was one of the Apostle Paul's prison epistles (*epistles* means "letters"). In the beginning of this letter, Paul made a bold statement about his priorities. He states that nothing, *nothing* can compare to knowing Jesus Christ. I imagine Paul had interests, things that excited him. But when he turned to Christ, he sold out. He gave up everything to follow God. Can you say the same thing?

We will all have our passions, our interests, our dreams, and our desires. But we must be willing to place them second to our devotion to Christ. Our love for knowing Christ, and getting to know Him more, must take precedence over all our other loves. (Yes, even baseball.)

Part of your identity as a Christ follower is being willing to pursue Him at all costs. Are you willing?

_____

_____

_____

_____

What interests you? What excites you more than anything?

_____

_____

_____

_____

Do you have a godly attitude about your interests? Do they get in the way of your devotion to Christ?

_____

_____

_____

_____

How can you use your interests and passions to serve Christ?

_____

_____

_____

_____

Verse 17

Do not conform to the pattern of this world, but be transformed by the renewing of your mind. Then you will be able to test and approve what God's will is—his good, pleasing and perfect will.

—Romans 12:2

L et's talks plastic. Many of you will drink out of some sort of a plastic bottle today. On the assembly line, the molds used to make the bottles serve as a *pattern*, making sure all the bottles are the same size and shape. It's pretty amazing actually. Picture millions of bottles all the exact same size, produced at the same time. Over and over again. They can be produced in such exacting detail because they make use of a pattern.

Read Romans 12:1–2. If you're like me, you've read these verses, written by the Apostle Paul, many times. These two verses have such a great deal to say about worship and transformation. But I don't know that I ever thought much about that little word, *pattern*. This little word is huge for us as we learn about our identities.

Look back at verse 2. Paul says to stop conforming to the pattern of this world. What does it mean to conform? Think about those plastic bottles we mentioned. When they are made, the plastic is heated up to a liquid state then poured into a mold (the pattern). The plastic conforms to the mold, taking the shape of the bottle. When you act like the world acts, you are conforming to its pattern. And Paul says this is a recipe for disaster. How do you keep from conforming? Transform yourself by turning your mind toward Christ. Focus on Him. His pattern is different from the world's. By conforming to *His* pattern, you identify yourself with other Christ followers, not world followers.

As you continue to learn about the nature of your identity, seek to be a person who is known for conforming to Christ.

Describe the pattern of the world around you. What values does culture say are important? What characteristics do you see being reinforced over and over?

_____

_____

_____

_____

Describe Christ's pattern. What does Jesus say is important? What characteristics and values do you see being reinforced by Christ over and over?

_____

_____

_____

_____

Describe the pressure you face to conform to this world. How can you rely on Christ to help you face the pressure?

_____

_____

_____

_____

Verse 18

Do your best to present yourself to God as one approved, a workman who does not need to be ashamed and who correctly handles the word of truth.

—2 Timothy 2:15

I used to work landscape installation. One day my boss sent me to Lowe's to pick up a hundred bags of shredded pine-bark *mulch*. We were building a playground; the mulch was so the kiddos wouldn't hurt themselves when they fell. Sounded like a great idea, except that I bought a hundred bags of pine bark *mini-nuggets*, which are about as soft as a cement mixer. We worked for two hours spreading the stuff on the ground. My boss pulled up and promptly lost his mind. It turned out to be about a $1,500 mistake on my part. Needless to say, it wasn't a great day.

Here's the key to the story: I meant well, but I goofed. It was Friday afternoon. I was thinking about the weekend. Not the work at hand. I wanted to please my boss, but my mistake showed I had a ways to go.

Read 2 Timothy 2:14–21. The books 1 and 2 Timothy are actually letters written by the Apostle Paul to his right-hand man, Timothy. Timothy was a young pastor and Paul's spiritual son. Paul was passing along fatherly type advice to Timothy on what it takes to be a leader in the church.

Look at verse 15. Paul said we should serve Christ like a worker serves their master. The worker's goal is to please their master, to show that he or she is a valuable, trustworthy, and an able worker. Paul is challenging us to serve Christ in a way that pleases God. Paul is commanding we "correctly" handle the things God has entrusted to us. While we know Christ has already earned our favor with God, we are still called to be diligent workers for Christ. This is a crucial part of your identity.

How do you serve God?

_____

_____

_____

What do you think it means to present yourself to God as one approved?

_____

_____

_____

What does it look like in your life to be a teenager who "correctly handles" God's Word? (Hint: I'm not talking about how you hold your Bible.)

_____

_____

_____

Do you ever think of yourself as a worker in Christ's kingdom? How does this image help you understand the call Jesus has given you to impact the world in His name?

_____

_____

_____

Verse 19

"Come, follow me," Jesus said, "and I will send you out to fish for people."

—Matthew 4:19

I've spent a lot of time around horses. I've worked on several ranches, here in my home state of Alabama and in Wyoming and Colorado. It's amazing to watch a horse that is not "broken," or trained. An unbroken horse is a thing of wild beauty. They are completely independent and as untamed as any wild animal can be. They are in total control. But something happens when they are trained. They become followers. The trainer takes a position of leadership. The horse follows the trainer's lead.

Read Matthew 4:18–22. This is the account of Jesus calling His first disciples. It was pretty straightforward in terms of a calling. Jesus pretty much said, "Hey guys. Drop the nets. Let's go." And they went. The disciples became followers.

Here's the interesting thing about followers. Think back to our horse example. Now just because a horse becomes a follower doesn't diminish its beauty or power. A horse is still a majestic, powerful creature. It's just allowed another individual to harness its power. In essence, the disciples did this when they became followers. Jesus harnessed their power to be used for His good. But He did something else too.

Jesus did more than harness the disciples' abilities. He changed their identity. In doing so, Jesus used imagery to describe this change. Look what He said in verse 19. He shifted the disciples' desire to gather fish and gave them the desire to gather souls. By committing to follow Jesus, the identity shift had begun. No longer would they fish to fill their bellies. They would forever fish to fill God's kingdom.

How has your identity changed since you decided to follow Christ?

_____

_____

_____

_____

Do you consider yourself a gatherer of souls? In what ways do you point people toward Christ?

_____

_____

_____

_____

What things have you left behind to follow Christ? If the answer is "none," don't you have to ask yourself if you are truly following Him?

_____

_____

_____

_____

Verse 20

You are the salt of the earth. But if the salt loses its saltiness, how can it be made salty again? It is no longer good for anything, except to be thrown out and trampled underfoot.

—Matthew 5:13

Do you like flavorful foods? For some people a bold meal is too much. It doesn't do it for them. But not me. I love Italian food: the rich cream sauces, the intricate spices. I also love Mexican food. It's tough to beat a steak burrito stuffed with jalapeños and onions and smothered in melted queso. And I love Chinese food. I lived in China for three months, and the food was unbelievable! Super spicy, with tons of wild textures we simply don't have in the States. (Excuse me . . . All of the sudden I'm crazy hungry.) The bolder the flavor, the better, I say.

Read Matthew 5:13–16, but not before I give you a warning: your identity is about to be transformed again. You see, in verse 13 Jesus compares His followers to salt. In Jesus' time salt had various uses. Certainly it was used to flavor food. But it was also used to preserve food; fisherman would cure their fish in salt so it would last longer. Salt was both a flavor additive and a preservative. Do you see the parallel yet between you, the Christ follower, and salt?

Jesus wanted His people to stand out in the world. Not because of their appearance, but because of their actions. Jesus also wanted His people to preserve the world through their actions. This is still His call to you today. He basically says, "You are to the world what salt is to food."

Jesus has made you into the world's salt. Because of your identity as a Christ follower, you are called to boldly make a difference. Live out your calling by making a difference in the world.

What does Jesus say in verse 15 about Christ followers who fail to make a difference in the world?

_____

_____

_____

_____

List some practical ways you are salt to the world around you.

_____

_____

_____

_____

Verse 21

Let us rejoice and be glad and give him glory! For the wedding of the Lamb has come, and his bride has made herself ready.

—Revelation 19:7

How many wedding movies have you seen? From sweet family-oriented types, like the *Mamma Mia* films or *My Big Fat Greek Wedding 1* and *2*, to "how bad can it get" comedies like *Bridesmaids*, audiences love them. Some years have more than others, but the bottom line is that Hollywood has never met a wedding it wouldn't make a movie out of.

Read Revelation 19:6–9. Now remember, the Book of Revelation is John's attempt to capture in words the amazing vision Jesus allowed him to see. John was in prison on the island of Patmos. While there, Jesus sent Him this vision in which John witnessed the end of the world and Jesus' triumphant second coming. What we see in this passage is the wedding banquet between Christ and His bride. Guess who the bride is? That's right . . . you're about to learn another image used to describe your identity in Christ.

You are the bride of Christ. Just as a bride gives herself over to one groom, waiting expectantly to be united with him, you will one day be united with Christ. All believers will be ushered to heaven to be presented to Jesus. Like a bride presented to her husband, you will come before Christ and celebrate with Him. And all Christ followers will join you, united in eternal fellowship with Jesus.

As you continue to learn about your identity in Christ, it's pretty cool to know that He is expecting you just as a groom awaits his bride.

Have you known anyone who has gotten married recently? How were they in the weeks and days leading up to the ceremony?

_____

_____

_____

_____

Do you live your life in a sense of expectation? Do you long for the day you will be united with Christ?

_____

_____

_____

_____

How should knowing what's coming affect your spiritual life on this earth?

_____

_____

_____

_____

Verse 22

Then Jesus said to his disciples, "Whoever wants to be my disciple must deny themselves and take up their cross and follow me."

—Matthew 16:24

The Congressional Medal of Honor is our country's highest military honor, given for extreme acts of bravery. Since it was first given out in 1861, only 3,505 people have been awarded the CMH. One of the more recent recipients was Ross Andrew McGinnis for the sacrifices he made in battle in Iraq. McGinnis was in the gun turret of an Army Humvee patrolling a neighborhood in Baghdad. Suddenly, an insurgent threw a grenade into the turret. McGinnis screamed "grenade," but in the cramped space of the Humvee, no one had time to move. In an instant, McGinnis dropped to the floor of the Humvee, absorbing the blast of the grenade with his body. In giving his life to protect his fellow soldiers, McGinnis saved four men. President George W. Bush awarded the medal to the McGinnis family in a ceremony at the White House.

Read Matthew 16:21–28. Pay special attention to verse 24. What does this verse have in common with the story about Ross McGinnis? One word: sacrifice. When Jesus says we are to deny ourselves and take up our cross if we want to follow Him, Jesus is talking all about sacrifice. Think of what the Cross was to Christ. It was the ultimate symbol of sacrifice. It was where God's very Son hung and died, punished for sins He never committed. Jesus was saying that His followers had to be willing to take up their crosses.

Jesus wants you to follow Him. To do so you must sacrifice those things that are in the way of you following in the path He set forth. Each person has a different cross. Only you know the things that get in the way of your relationship with the Lord.

Are you willing to be known as a person who makes sacrifices for the sake of following Christ?

_____

_____

_____

What is your cross? What is that one thing standing in the way of totally following after Christ?

_____

_____

_____

What do you think it means to deny yourself?

_____

_____

_____

Write a prayer to the Holy Spirit asking Him to empower you to follow Christ. Ask for the strength to sacrifice those things that stand in your way.

_____

_____

_____

Verse 23

For God so loved the world that he gave his one and only Son, that whoever believes in him shall not perish but have eternal life.

—John 3:16

Read John 3:16–21. While John 3:16 is probably a pretty familiar passage to you, I hope you learned something new reading the surrounding passages.

But I want to focus for a moment on John 3:16. I want you to look at it a little differently today. I want you to look at it in terms of how it relates to your identity in Christ. This is a really cool exchange where Jesus talks about polar opposites, namely, life and death.

Most of us think a lot about those two things. What will our lives be like? Who will we love, and what will we wind up doing for a career? What will the world be like when we're 30 or 50 or 70? How long will we live? What happens when we die? It's natural for us to wonder about the coming years, even if the unknown is more than a tad frightening.

But because you are a Christ follower, you have been given a great gift. Christ transformed you from a dead person to a living person. You were dead in your sins. But on the Cross, Jesus gave you life. When you think about how that affects your identity, it is pretty simple: you can live as one who is assured a future, a life after this one. And this future life will last forever in the presence of God. Can you imagine a greater gift?

List some ways your life as a Christ follower (someone who is "living") should be different from someone who does not believe in Christ.

_____

_____

_____

_____

How does it make you feel when you think about the gift of eternal life Christ purchased for you?

_____

_____

_____

_____

Verse 24

I am the vine; you are the branches. If you remain in me and I in you, you will bear much fruit; apart from me you can do nothing.

—John 15:5

Do something for me: I want you to go over to your game console and unplug it. Go ahead. I'll wait. Great. Now, press the power button, grab a controller, and . . . nothing. Do the same thing with your TV. Go unplug it from the power strip. Now, plop down on the couch, grab the remote, click the power button, and . . . what gives? Why won't your stuff work? Okay, dumb question. Obviously you know the answer. But do you see my point? Your game console or your TV must be connected to a power source for it to work. It doesn't matter how badly you want to watch whichever show you're binging this week or play a game. Without power, you've got nothing.

Read John 15:5–8. Jesus was talking to His disciples in one of their last moments together before His arrest, trial, and Crucifixion. Jesus was using the imagery of a vine, probably a grape vine, to teach His disciples about the source of their power. He explained it this way: Jesus is like the main trunk of a grape vine. His disciples are like the vines that grow out from the trunk; as long as they stay attached, they will produce fruit. However, if the branches are detached, they will not produce fruit. When Jesus said "fruit," he meant the good deeds that come as a result of our faith.

On your own you might try to be good, but you, like all people, are naturally inclined to look out for yourself first, others second. If you remain in the vine of Christ, your identity will be that of a branch; you will be attached to Christ.

Just like a power source powers a TV, Jesus will power you. He will enable you to live righteously and bring glory and honor to Him.

Are you living like a branch connected to the Vine? Or as one that has been paired away?

_____

_____

_____

_____

If we apply this parable, we would agree that the proof of our closeness to Christ is in our fruit—our godly actions. What do your actions say about your relationship with Christ?

_____

_____

_____

_____

What changes can you make in your life to more closely identify you with the Vine?

_____

_____

_____

_____

Verse 25

This, then, is how you ought to regard us: as servants of Christ and as those entrusted with the mysteries God has revealed.

—1 Corinthians 4:1

What images come to mind when you think of the word *servant*? I think of a tuxedo-clad dude with perfect posture, an English accent, a pencil-thin mustache, and a name like "Henderson," as in, "Henderson, go tell the cook we'll be hosting the polo club for dinner this evening." The second image that comes to mind is some sort of medieval servant groveling in a dark castle as an unruly king barks orders while drinking mead out of a goblet and eating a giant turkey leg. Okay, so it's obvious I either A) watch too many movies, or B) have a vivid imagination. But you get my drift, right? In the American culture that puts so much emphasis on freedom and independence, the idea of a servant is kind of distasteful and foreign.

Read 1 Corinthians 4:1–2. Paul, teaching the Corinthians what it means to be a follower of Christ, set up the metaphor of servant and master. In the Roman culture, even poor people had servants. The Roman armies would conquer other nations and bring their inhabitants back to Rome as servants and slaves. Many of these servants would work in the homes of Roman citizens. The idea of servanthood was one Paul's audience could easily relate to.

Paul was calling us to live as servants in Christ's house. We are to look to Him as master. Our desire should be to serve Christ in a trustworthy manner. He has given us so much; we are called simply to serve Him. And we should gladly do so out of our love and appreciation. After all, Christ set the example of service, living a life of service while on this earth. And who could ask for a better master?

Your goal should be to live in such a way that your identity is defined by your service to Christ.

In your own words, what does it mean to serve Christ in your world each day?

_____

_____

_____

_____

God has blessed you in so many ways. How can you prove that you are trustworthy in using your blessings for His glory?

_____

_____

_____

_____

Write a short prayer to God professing your desire to serve Him.

_____

_____

_____

_____

Verse 26

Now you are the body of Christ, and each one of you is a part of it.

—1 Corinthians 12:27

Think for a moment the last time you worked together with a group to achieve a common goal. Maybe it was a cheerleading squad or a volleyball team. Or maybe it had nothing to do with sports. Maybe it was a band concert or school play. Maybe you worked with a couple friends to write the code for a cool app. Or maybe you built a website with some buddies. Whatever the case, if you did anything similar to these tasks, you combined your talents with those of other people to achieve something greater than you could have achieved on your own. It's a pretty amazing concept if you think about it.

Read 1 Corinthians 12:14–27. This passage has a ton to say about your identity as a Christ follower. Do you get what is going on? The Apostle Paul is comparing believers to a body. Just like your body is made up of all kinds of parts that have unique purposes, the church body is made up of Christ followers who are all gifted by God in unique ways. And when believers work together, they can do amazing things.

The image of you as a part of a body is pretty remarkable. It totally reframes your purpose, doesn't it? It shifts the focus from you as an individual to you as a part of a larger plan with a larger purpose. You are a valuable part of the church—the body of Christ on this earth. That is truly a major piece of your identity.

But it doesn't stop there. Just like the eleven players on a football team can work together to accomplish more than any one person could, you can work together with other Christ followers to use your gifts to change the world. Are you using what God has given you for His purposes?

What are the different talents or passions God has gifted you with?

_____

_____

_____

_____

In what ways do you use these talents for the purposes of serving the church?

_____

_____

_____

_____

How does knowing you are part of the body of Christ change the way you look at your identity?

_____

_____

_____

_____

Verse 27

For we are to God the pleasing aroma of Christ among those who are being saved and those who are perishing.

—2 Corinthians 2:15

What are your favorite smells? I've got a pretty long list. I love the smell of barbecue slow cooking on a real, hardwood fire. I love the smell of a baseball park, and it doesn't matter if it's little league, minor league, college, or the pros; the combination of hotdogs, popcorn, and freshly cut grass will always be a sign of summer. My wife used to wear this one kind of perfume when we were dating. It ran out sometime early on in our marriage, and she never replaced it. To this day, if a woman walks past me wearing that brand of perfume, I am instantly carried back to a time when my wife and I were mere kids, just barely starting out in our life together.

Read 2 Corinthians 2:14–17. There are actually a few different things working here. Don't be thrown off by the "triumphal procession" remark. Paul is using an image from Roman culture. When the Romans would conquer a foreign army, they would parade back through Rome (hence, a triumphal procession) so the victorious generals could be celebrated. But I want to focus on what Paul said about us being like a fragrant aroma. Because in terms of your identity, it's a pretty cool concept.

Just like a pleasing aroma or smell spreads through a crowd, we are responsible for spreading the knowledge of Christ. Some will see Christ in us, and it will be like a pleasing smell. They might be attracted to it. They just might want to know more.

You are tasked with the responsibility of being the sweet fragrance of Christ. The people around you will not have the chance to respond positively to the message of Christ if you do not commit to being a fragrant aroma.

List some practical ways in which you are a pleasing aroma of Christ to the world around you.

_____

_____

_____

_____

How does the idea of being like a sweet fragrance to God change the way you look at your identity?

_____

_____

_____

_____

Are you comfortable spreading around the knowledge of Christ? Or do you struggle demonstrating your faith? What can you do to become more comfortable?

_____

_____

_____

_____

Verse 28

For we are God's handiwork, created in Christ Jesus to do good works, which God prepared in advance for us to do.

—Ephesians 2:10

Stop and think for a moment about objects and their purposes. Just about any object you see was created by someone for some purpose. Currently I am writing this devotion in my kitchen. If I look up, I see a lamp designed by someone with the purpose of providing light. I see a bowl. This one is a little different. It was actually made by my brother, an artist and potter, so my wife could have something to put fruit in. Across the way I see one of my favorite objects. It is a coffee maker, created by the fine people at Braun with the expressed purpose of providing me with coffee each morning. They have no idea how much I love them for that. Look around you. What objects do you see? What is their purpose?

Read Ephesians 2:1–10. Paul was writing from prison in Rome to the church in Ephesus. Here, Paul is talking about the amazing grace God extended to humankind through His Son, Jesus. Paul talks about the sense of ownership God has for us, how He longs to lavish us with praise. In verse 10 we learn the nature of our relationship to God and the purpose for which He designed us.

God looks at you as His treasured creation. You are His handiwork. This means to the world you are evidence of God's great compassion, love, and power. And you were created by Him to do what? Good works in Christ Jesus. Your purpose is to live out Christ's teachings in this world. You are called to act rightly.

How amazing is it that your identity testifies to the world of God's creative hand? Praise God for His grace, love, and desire to have you be a part of His plan.

Part of your identity is this idea of being God's handiwork, the fruit of His creative labor. How does this make you feel?

_____

_____

_____

_____

When you think about applying this verse in your life, what are some ways you demonstrate good works in the world around you?

_____

_____

_____

_____

Write a prayer asking God to show you opportunities today to do good works in His name.

_____

_____

_____

_____

Verse 29

For you were once darkness, but now you are light
in the Lord. Live as children of light.

—Ephesians 5:8

When I was a child my father worked for a university. The school sponsored a weekend cave-exploring trip, and my dad allowed me to tag along. This was a real-deal, underground cave that stretched for miles and miles. I couldn't have been six years old, so it was quite an adventure; I had my own helmet and headlamp and everything. (In hindsight, my dad must have been nuts!) I will never forget shuffling along in the dark, damp cavern with my father and a dozen or so college students.

I remember entering into this one cavern where the narrow passageways gave way to an expansive cathedral-sized room. It seemed as though we had stepped out into space. Everyone was looking around, their headlamps illuminating the sky-high ceiling. Then we all decided to turn off our lights to see how dark it was. Let me tell you, if you've never been cave exploring, you've never known darkness like this. It was suffocating. I remember feeling paralyzed until someone cut his headlamp on. And suddenly light exploded through the darkness. One by one the lamps went on. The room was illuminated, the darkness dispelled.

Read Ephesians 5:8–14. What great imagery. Paul told the Ephesians that while they once lived in darkness (the darkness of their sin), they now live in light . . . the wonderful light of Christ. What does it mean to live as light in this world? Paul gives the answer in verse 13. We are to expose the sinful darkness of the world by reflecting the light of Christ.

Like a headlamp cutting through a dark cavern, your identity is tied to being light in a dark world. Are you up to the task?

_____

_____

_____

_____

Do you see spiritual darkness in the world around you? List some examples.

_____

_____

_____

_____

List some ways you are able to shine the light of Christ in your world.

_____

_____

_____

_____

How could you improve your reflectivity? In other words, in what ways could you do a better job of reflecting Christ's love as you go about your daily life?

_____

_____

_____

_____

Verse 30

But if we walk in the light, as he is in the light, we have fellowship with one another, and the blood of Jesus, his Son, purifies us from all sin.

—1 John 1:7

Do you know what a conditional statement is? Well, let's break it down. What is a *condition*? A condition is a stipulation of a contract, a basic idea or rule that is essential to an agreement. For example, a condition of an inmate's parole might be good behavior. Got it? Now, you know what a *statement* is . . . no need to go into a lot of depth there. When you put the two together you get: a statement communicating a condition. You're actually pretty familiar with this idea. Here's one you've probably heard: "If you don't pass your chemistry exam, you will not get to go to the prom." Or, "If you want to live to see seventeen, you better not get another speeding ticket." Yup, you're familiar with them. And now that you know what to look for, you'll see conditional statements all around you.

Read 1 John 1:5–10. John loved to use metaphors. (See the little book entitled Revelation.) While they can sometimes make his writings tricky to apply, John's metaphors give us such wonderful pictures of the things of God. This passage is no different. What a wonderful image: God is light. In Him there is no darkness. John says if we say we love God, we better be light too. Pretty simple. Yet pretty profound.

Look closely at verse 7. Here we see John the Apostle giving us a pretty cool conditional statement. He says that if we want fellowship with one another and Christ, we must do what? What is the condition? That's right: we must walk in the light. That's another awesome picture of your identity in Christ . . . you are a light walker!

Stay true to your identity. Commit to walking in the light today.

If sin and evil are defined as darkness, what does John mean by the light?

_____

_____

_____

_____

Think for a moment about those dark places that tempt you. Are there some practical things you can do to stay away from them?

_____

_____

_____

_____

How are you leading others toward the light?

_____

_____

_____

_____

Verse 31

However, I consider my life worth nothing to me; my only aim is to finish the race and complete the task the Lord Jesus has given me—the task of testifying to the good news of God's grace.

—Acts 20:24

I can't stand quitting. I don't care how tough a situation or a task gets, quitting is always the absolute last option. I remember eighth grade basketball. I made the team and after three games was the leading scorer. But the coach and I didn't see eye-to-eye. So he started benching me. No matter how hard I worked, it made no difference. Looking back, I share some of the blame. I was a little conceited. But I still have no idea why he stopped playing me. Oh, how I wanted to quit. But my mom made me stick it out. I learned a valuable lesson, one that has stuck with me the rest of my life. I can count on one hand the number of things I have flat-out quit. I'm just not a quitter.

Paul was no quitter either. Read Acts 20:22–24. Let's be honest: Paul was a straight-up stud. I mean, he had been through it all. He had suffered as much as any one person could for the sake of Jesus Christ. Yet look at his resolve. He knew he had a calling. And that calling was sharing the story of

Christ with the world. Only death would stop him, and in the end, that was the only thing that could.

I want to challenge you to be like Paul. Don't give up. Live for Christ. Stand against the world! Don't ever compromise your beliefs. And through it all, never, ever quit. If you are living like you should, it won't be easy. But if you trust in the Spirit to guide you, you will be able to persevere.

Fight the good fight. Finish the race. Be identified as a person of God.

Have you ever wanted to quit something but ended up sticking it out? What did you learn from your experience?

_____

_____

_____

_____

How do your decisions and attitudes show what you value most? Do you value your own interests more than you value God's call to make Himself known?

_____

_____

_____

_____

Closing

Wow . . . I was wondering if you'd see it through. And here you are. Good for you.

I wish I could talk to you. I wish I could ask you what you thought. Not about my writing or even the book itself. I am most curious to know your reaction to what you learned from Scripture. As I wrote this book, over and over again I was amazed at God's love for us. I hope I always will be.

So what *did* you think? Did you like it? Did you learn anything?

Maybe you knew most of this stuff. Maybe you're one of those teenagers who just gets it. And if you do, that is so awesome. Chances are, you're a little ahead of the game right now. But God doesn't look at things that way. You are called to seek Him with all you are. My message to you is to keep growing, keep seeking, keep living your life for Christ.

Then again, maybe you are like I was in high school. When I was your age, I had not yet committed my life to following Christ. I had such huge questions about who I was, whether or not my life mattered, and what my future held for me. I wish I had known even a portion of the truths contained in God's Word. Knowing my identity in Christ would have saved me from so much.

My prayer is this book has revealed God's truth to you in a way you had not previously known. My prayer is that encountering Christ in a new way has changed you. I wish I could hear you tell me how you were changed. Maybe we'll run into each other some day. I look forward to it.

How to Become a Christian

You're not here by accident. God loves you. He wants you to have a personal relationship with Him through Jesus, His Son. There is just one thing that separates you from God. That one thing is sin.

The Bible describes sin in many ways. Most simply, sin is our failure to measure up to God's holiness and His righteous standards. We sin by things we do, choices we make, attitudes we show, and thoughts we entertain. We also sin when we fail to do right things. The Bible affirms our own experience— "there is no one righteous, not even one" (Romans 3:10). No matter how good we try to be, none of us does right things all the time.

People tend to divide themselves into groups—good people and bad people. But God says every person who has ever lived is a sinner, and any sin separates us from God. No matter how we might classify ourselves, this includes you and me. We are all sinners.

For all have sinned and fall short of the glory of God.

—Romans 3:23

Many people are confused about the way to God. Some think they will be punished or rewarded according to how good they are. Some think they should make things right in their lives before they try to come to God. Others find it hard to understand how Jesus could love them when other people don't seem to. But I have great news for you! God *does* love you! More than you can ever imagine! And there's nothing you can do to make Him stop! Yes, our sins demand punishment— the punishment of death and separation from God. But because of His great love, God sent His only Son Jesus to die for our sins.

> But God demonstrates his own love for us in this:
> While we were still sinners, Christ died for us.
>
> —Romans 5:8

For you to come to God, you have to get rid of your sin problem. But not one of us can do this in our own strength! You can't make yourself right with God by being a better person. Only God can rescue us from our sins. He is willing to do this not because of anything you can offer Him, but *just because He loves you!*

> He saved us, not because of righteous things we had done, but because of His mercy.
>
> —Titus 3:5

It's God's grace that allows you to come to Him—not your efforts to "clean up your life" or work your way to heaven. You can't earn it. It's a free gift.

> For it is by grace you have been saved, through faith—and this is not from yourselves, it is the gift of God—not by works, so that no one can boast.
>
> —Ephesians 2:8–9

For you to come to God, the penalty for your sin must be paid. God's gift to you is His Son Jesus, who paid the debt for you when He died on the Cross.

> For the wages of sin is death, but the gift of God is eternal life in Christ Jesus our Lord.
>
> —Romans 6:23

Jesus paid the price for your sin and mine by giving His life on a Cross at a place called Calvary, just outside of the city walls of Jerusalem in ancient Israel. God brought Jesus back from the dead. He provided the way for you to have a personal relationship with Him through Jesus. When we realize how deeply our sin grieves the heart of God and how desperately we need a Savior, we are ready to receive God's offer of salvation. To admit we are sinners means turning away from our sin and selfishness and turning to follow Jesus. The Bible's word for this is *repentance*—to change our thinking about how grievous sin is, so our thinking is in line with God's.

All that's left for you to do is to accept the gift that Jesus is holding out for you right now.

If you declare with your mouth, "Jesus is Lord," and believe in your heart that God raised him from the dead, you will be saved. For it is with your heart that you believe and are justified, and it is with your mouth that you profess your faith and are saved.

—Romans 10:9–10

God says that if you believe in His Son Jesus, you can live forever with Him in glory.

For God so loved the world that He gave his one and only Son, that whoever believes in him shall not perish but have eternal life.

—John 3:16

Are you ready to accept the gift of eternal life Jesus is offering you right now? Let's review what this commitment involves:

- I acknowledge I am a sinner in need of a Savior—this is to repent or turn away from sin.
- I believe in my heart that God raised Jesus from the dead—this is to trust that Jesus paid the full penalty for my sins.
- I confess Jesus as my Lord and my God—this is to surrender control of my life to Jesus.
- I receive Jesus as my Savior forever—this is to accept that God has done for me and in me what He promised.

If it is your sincere desire to receive Jesus into your heart as your personal Lord and Savior, then talk to God from your heart.

Here's a suggested prayer:

"Lord Jesus, I know I am a sinner, and I do not deserve eternal life. But I believe You died and rose from the grave to make me a new creation and to prepare me to dwell in Your presence forever. Jesus, come into my life, take control of my life, forgive my sins, and save me. I am now placing my trust in You alone for my salvation, and I accept your free gift of eternal life. Amen."

How to Share Your Faith

When engaging someone with the gospel, we use the same approach we see Jesus using in Scripture: love, listen, discern, and respond.

Love
Love comes from God
Go out of your way
Go be amongst the crowd
Change your environment

Listen
Ask questions
Listen for the heart issue
Don't defend or argue

Discern

Discernment is from the Holy Spirit
Discern the Holy Spirit's leading
What's the point of entry?

Respond

When we love, listen, and discern, we are prepared to respond, the Holy Spirit does the work, and God is glorified.

Ask, "Is there anything keeping you from accepting the free gift of life in Jesus today?"

You can help your friend pray to receive salvation by praying the prayer on page 68.

How to Pray for Your Friends

God is a creator. He doesn't make mistakes. He loves making beauty from ashes and turning strength from fear. When people accept Him as their Savior, He makes them new beings. If one of your friends is still living in their old nature, ask God to help make them new.

God, I know you want to make beautiful things. Creation shows me Your power and beauty, and Your Word says You want to make us new creatures. Help my friend _____ today to shake off their old sinful nature and to walk in the newness of life with You. God, make _____ a new creature. Amen.

Genesis tells us we are made in the image of God. We are a reflection of Him and His nature to the world around us.

God, I know _____ follows after You. Help him/her be a reflection of You today in the world around us. Help him/her to shine brightly for You so our friends who believe are encouraged to walk deeper in their faith and our friends who don't believe see something that attracts them to You. Amen.

As a Christ follower, it is important to clothe yourself in Christ. Pray for your friends today that they too can be clothed in Christ through their actions:

Jesus, You are the one who clothes me in righteousness (right standing with God), so help me and _____ be clothed in You today. Help us choose to follow You so our attitudes, words, and actions honor You. We need help with _____(Insert a specific need. Examples: self-control when we want to lose it with someone; restraint not to talk about others; patience with siblings who get on our nerves; boldness to stand up for you, etc.)

**If you enjoyed this book, will you consider
sharing the message with others?**

Let us know your thoughts at info@newhopepublishers.com.
You can also let the author know by visiting or sharing a photo
of the cover on our social media pages or leaving a review at a
retailer's site. All of it helps us get the message out!

Twitter.com/NewHopeBooks
Facebook.com/NewHopePublishers
Instagram.com/NewHopePublishers

————————————

New Hope® Publishers is an imprint
of Iron Stream Media, which derives
its name from Proverbs 27:17,
"As iron sharpens iron, so one
person sharpens another."

This sharpening describes the process of discipleship, one to
another. With this in mind, Iron Stream Media provides a variety
of solutions for churches, missionaries, and nonprofits ranging
from in-depth Bible study curriculum and Christian book
publishing to custom publishing and consultative services.
Through the popular Life Bible Study and Student Life Bible Study
brands, ISM provides web-based full-year and short-term Bible
study teaching plans as well as printed devotionals, Bibles,
and discipleship curriculum.

For more information on ISM and
New Hope Publishers, please visit
IronStreamMedia.com
NewHopePublishers.com